SMART BOOKS FOR KIDS

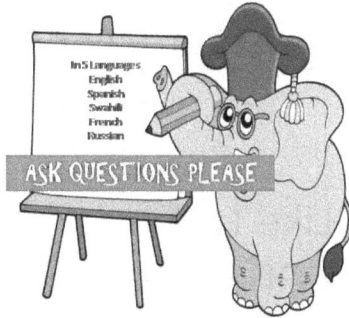

In 5 Languages
English
Spanish
Swahili
French
Russian

ASK QUESTIONS PLEASE

English-Español-Kiswahili-Français-Pyccкий

Ask Questions
Please

466 TO 470 OF 700

Educational Books

5 Books In 1 In 5 Languages

English, Spanish, Swahili, French & Russian

ACKNOWLEDGEMENT

I Would Like To Acknowledge The
CREATOR OF HEAVEN AND EARTH
(GOD) FOR ALL THAT HE HAS Given
Me. Thanking God I Am For My Talents
and Gifts.
I Recognize That The Lord Gave Me
This Gift, Which Allows Me To Share
With Children And Everyone That
Participates In The Reading Of The
Literary Material That I Produce
Through The Commission Of God.

Thank You Lord God

I Will Forever Be Grateful
For Your Trust In Me

Pamela Denise Brown
Goodwill Ambassador
For The Positive Cultivation
Of Children

My EDUCATIONAL Collection Of Books Are For The
Advancement Of Children.
I'm Not Selling Books, I Am However, Providing Thought
Leading Reinforcements, That Can Be Simplistically Utilized
As Reference Material, As An Investment In The Positive
Cultivation Of Children's Lives.

A little information about the author, My Educational Books are designed to educate children, to transform the way a child thinks, to better children so they can become successful people. I write educational books to help children develop and grow psychologically.

As an Ambassador for the cultivation of children, I am a trusted source moving to inspire children with innovative ideas, creating evolutionary advancements by urging children to be open to new ways of thinking.

I present children with an opportunity to replicate and scale the ideas from the pages of the educational literature I produce into sustainable change, by shaping the lives of children from any background, community, age, ethnicity or gender. My goal is to give children balance and broaden their understanding as it relates to "co-existing" in society as a coherent whole.

I have codified what I know and placed it within reach. I am strategically reaching into the mind of every child that reads the literary information that I have produced in my Collection of Educational Books.

Books Speak For You books may be ordered through booksellers or by contacting:
Booksspeakforyou.com
The views expressed in this work are solely those of the author.
Any illustration provided by iStock and such images are being used for illustrative purposes.
Certain stock imagery © iStock.
ISBN:1640503617
Library of Congress Control Number:
Printed in the United States Of America

THE BOOKS

700 BOOKS IN 60 DAYS

I was commissioned by God to first write 40 Books in 40 days, then 100 books in 100 days on October 1, 2015, which I completed on January 8, 2016, commissioned again June 7, 2016 to write 700 books in 60 days starting July, 2016.

INTRODUCTION

My Collection Of EDUCATIONAL Books are designed to foster the social development of children psychologically. My books are designed to teach children values, morals and reintroduce manners to them. I believe the books I write will transform the minds of children, which ultimately will cause them to pause, to think and make better choices.

My EDUCATIONAL Books are designed to effectuate change and influence success in the lives of every child.

The EDUCATIONAL Books in the Collection are Reinforcements to Learning.

My EDUCATIONAL books will help build children's self-esteem and confidence to a level that will help them socially engage in a diverse world with confidence and harmony and ultimately prepare them for life.

Children Stand silently trying to open a door that cannot
be opened with hands...
Written 11/23/2015 11:18 a.m.

If to educate is your objective than to learn is your AIM...
Written 11/21/2015 1:41 a.m.

With Even Strokes Caress The Mind,
With Gentle Words Handle A Child,
With Excitement Finish The Race,
With Commitment Help A Child
Stay In Place.
LOVE IS EVERLASTING WITH GOD.
Written: July 3, 2016 @ 10:06 pm.

If you really want to enhance the life of a child, your first
step is to see yourself like a child and then approach the
child like you see yourself.
Written: 11/21/2015 2:22 a.m.

If You're In A "CROWDED" Room and A Child Is Sitting
"ALONE" That Can Only Mean The Room Is EMPTY...
Written 11/21/2015 1:42 a.m.

SMART BOOKS FOR KIDS

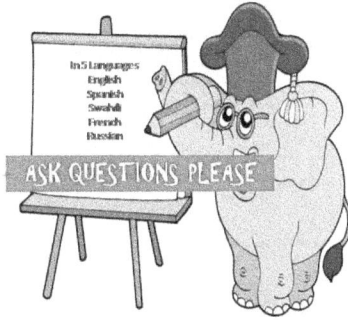

In 5 Languages
English
Spanish
Swahili
French
Russian

ASK QUESTIONS PLEASE

English-Español-Kiswahili-Français-Русский

ASK QUESTIONS

PLEASE

ENGLISH

466

Lois McNeil was a law Professor at Widespread Law School where she taught Environmental Law.

Often after her many lectures, Lois would ask the class, if they had questions. Most of the time, Lois's class would harmoniously answer NO.

This sometimes bothered Lois, as she knew herself being a law student once, that there were hundreds of times when she did not fully understand what was lectured to her, it was by asking questions Lois was able to finally comprehend the lesson.

NO questions, before we move on, Lois repeatedly asked.

There was a moment of silence, which indicated no one had anything to say.

Then all of a sudden, the young man sitting in the back of the class, raised his hand and said,
I have a question.

Finally, Lois replied.
I was beginning to think I was in a room full of geniuses that knew it all.

I'm glad to know that I'm needed, Lois said.
How may I help you Mr. Porter, Lois asked.

Mr. Porter began to ask his question.

After Mr. Porter asked his question, some of the other students spoke out at the same time and said,
I was going to ask that same question.
Lois answered, Mr. Porter's question.   Afterwards Lois asked the class again.

Does anyone have any questions?

This time several students raised their hands eager to ask Lois a question.

As Lois concluded, she reiterated her statement and said to the class Ask Questions Please, because in asking questions you gain knowledge and understanding.

WORKBOOK SECTION

Children Do You Think It's Important To Ask Questions And Why?

_____
_____
_____
_____
_____
_____
_____
_____
_____
_____
_____
_____

Why Do You Think Children Hold Their Questions In And When Someone Else Asks A Question They Wanted To Ask, They Yell Out, "I Was Going To Ask That Question"

._____
_____
_____
_____
_____
_____
_____

Do You Have A Fear Of Asking Questions? Or Do You Believe Your Teacher Won't Think Your Question Is Valuable?

_____
_____
_____
_____
_____
_____
_____
_____
_____
_____
_____

Do You Believe If You Ask More Questions You'll Understand Your Lesson Better?

_____
_____
_____
_____
_____
_____
_____
_____
_____

What If Anything Keeps You From Asking Your Teacher Questions During Class? And Or Does Your Teacher Give You An Opportunity To Ask Questions?

_____

_____

_____

_____

_____

_____

_____

_____

Take A Minute And Think About A Subject You May Have Difficulty In And Think Of A Question That You Might Want to Ask That Will Give you A Better Understanding Of The Subject. Write The Question In the Provided Space Below And Then Ask The Question.

_____

_____

_____

_____

_____

_____

_____

_____

_____

_____

_____

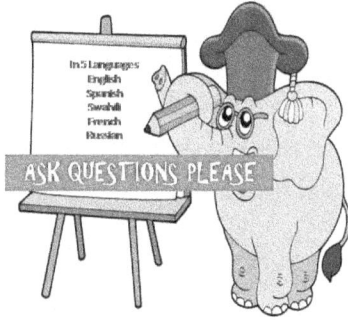

In 5 Languages
English
Spanish
Swahili
French
Russian

ASK QUESTIONS PLEASE

English-Español-Kiswahili-Français-Русский

ASK QUESTIONS

PLEASE

SPANISH

467

Lois McNeil fue profesora de derecho en la Facultad de Derecho de Widespread donde enseñó Derecho Ambiental.

A menudo, después de sus numerosas conferencias, Lois preguntaba a la clase si tenían preguntas.

La mayor parte del tiempo, la clase de Lois respondería armoniosamente NO.

Esto a veces molestó a Lois, ya que sabía que era una estudiante de derecho una vez, que había cientos de veces cuando ella no entendía completamente lo que se le enseñó, fue haciendo preguntas que Lois pudo finalmente comprender la lección.

No hay preguntas, antes de seguir adelante, Lois repetidamente preguntó.

Hubo un momento de silencio, que indicaba que nadie tenía nada que decir.

De repente, el joven sentado en la parte de atrás de la clase, levantó la mano y dijo:

Tengo una pregunta.

Finalmente, Lois respondió.

Empezaba a pensar que estaba en una habitación llena de genios que lo sabían todo.

-Me alegro de saber que me hacen falta -dijo Lois.

¿Cómo puedo ayudarlo, Sr. Porter? -preguntó Lois.

El Sr. Porter comenzó a hacer su pregunta.

Después de que el Sr. Porter hizo su pregunta, algunos de los otros estudiantes hablaron al mismo tiempo y dijeron:

Iba a hacer la misma pregunta.

Lois contestó la pregunta del señor Porter. Después Lois le preguntó a la clase otra vez.

¿Alguien tiene alguna pregunta?

Esta vez, varios estudiantes levantaron las manos ansiosos por preguntarle a Lois.

Como Lois concluyó, ella reiteró su declaración y dijo a la clase. Haga preguntas por favor, porque al hacer preguntas usted obtiene conocimiento y comprensión.

In 5 Languages
English
Spanish
Swahili
French
Russian

ASK QUESTIONS PLEASE

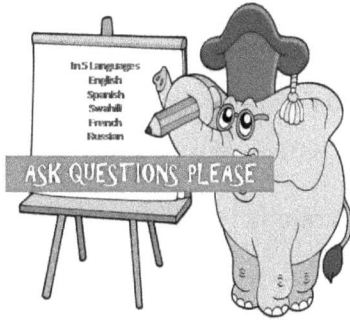

English-Español-Kiswahili-Français-Русский

ASK QUESTIONS

PLEASE

SWAHILI

468

Lois McNeil ilikuwa sheria Profesa katika Kuenea Law School ambapo yeye kufundisha Sheria ya Mazingira.

Mara nyingi baada ya mihadhara yake mengi, Lois bila kuuliza darasani, kama walikuwa na maswali.

Zaidi ya muda, daraja la Lois ingekuwa umoja kujibu NO.

This wakati mwingine bothered Lois, kama yeye mwenyewe alijua kuwa mwanafunzi wa sheria mara moja, kwamba kulikuwa na mamia ya nyakati wakati yeye hakuwa na kuelewa nini ilikuwa alihadhiri na yake, ilikuwa kwa kuuliza maswali Lois alikuwa na uwezo wa hatimaye kuelewa somo.

maswali NO, kabla ya sisi kuondoka, Lois kurudia aliuliza.

There ilikuwa wakati wa ukimya, ambazo zilionyesha hakuna mtu alikuwa na kitu chochote cha kusema.

Kisha kwa ghafla, kijana ameketi katika nyuma ya darasa, akainua mkono wake na akasema,

I una swali.

Hatimaye, Lois alijibu.

Nilikuwa mwanzo nadhani alikuwa katika chumba kamili ya akili maalum kwamba anajua yote.

I'm furaha kwa kujua kwamba mimi nina inahitajika, Lois alisema.

Jinsi naomba kukusaidia Mheshimiwa Porter, Lois aliuliza.

Mheshimiwa Porter alianza kuuliza swali lake.

Baada ya Mheshimiwa Porter aliuliza swali lake, baadhi ya wanafunzi wengine alizungumza nje wakati huo huo na kusema,

Mimi nilikuwa kwenda kuuliza swali hilo hilo.

Lois akajibu, swali Mheshimiwa Porter ya. Baada ya hapo Lois aliuliza darasa tena.

Je, mtu yeyote una maswali yoyote?

Wakati huu wanafunzi kadhaa kunyanyua mikono yao hamu ya kuuliza swali Lois.

AS Lois alihitimisha, yeye alielezea kauli yake na kusema kwa darasa Uliza maswali Tafadhali, kwa sababu katika kuuliza maswali wewe kupata maarifa na ufahamu.

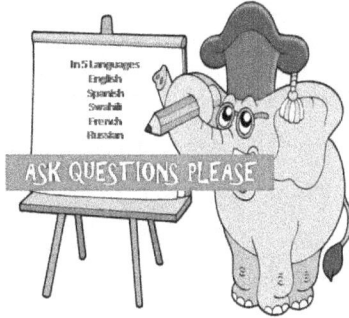

In 5 Languages
English
Spanish
Swahili
French
Russian

ASK QUESTIONS PLEASE

English-Español-Kiswahili-Français-Русский

ASK QUESTIONS

PLEASE

RUSSIAN

469

Lois McNeil byl zakon professor Widespread Yuridicheskoy shkoly, gde ona prepodavala ekologicheskogo prava.

Chasto posle togo, kak yeye mnogo lektsiy, Lois budet prosit' klass, yesli u nikh yest' voprosy.
Bol'shuyu chast' vremeni, klass Lois by garmonichno otvetit' NET.

Eta inogda bespokoili Lois, tak kak ona znala, chto sama buduchi studentom yuridicheskogo fakul'teta odnazhdy, chto sushchestvuyut sotni raz, kogda ona ne v polnoy mere ponyat', chto lektsii yey, eto, zadavaya voprosy Lois smog, nakonets, ponyat' urok.
Nikakikh voprosov, prezhde chem dvigat'sya dal'she, Lois mnogokratno prosili.

There byl moment molchaniya, chto ukazyvalo nikto ne imel nichego skazat'.

Potom vdrug, molodoy chelovek, sidyashchiy v zadney chasti klassa, podnyal ruku i skazal:

I yest' vopros.
I, nakonets, Lois otvetil.

YA nachal dumat', chto ya byl v komnate, polnoy geniyev,
kotoryye znali vse.

I'm rad uznat', chto ya nuzhen, skazal Lois.
Kak ya mogu vam pomoch' g-n Porter, poprosil Lois.
G-n Porter nachal zadavat' svoy vopros.

Posle togo, kak g-n Porter zadal svoy vopros, nekotoryye iz
drugikh studentov vystupali v to zhe vremya i skazal,
YA sobiralsya zadat' tot zhe samyy vopros.
Lois otvetil na vopros g-Porter. Zatem Lois snova sprosil
klass.

Kto-nibud' yest' kakiye-libo voprosy?

Na etot raz neskol'ko studentov podnyali ruki,
zhazhdushchikh zadat' Lois vopros.

AS Lois prishel k vyvodu, chto ona povtorila svoye
zayavleniye i skazal k klassu zadavat' voprosy, pozhaluysta,
potomu chto v zadavat' voprosy vy poluchite znaniya i
ponimaniye.

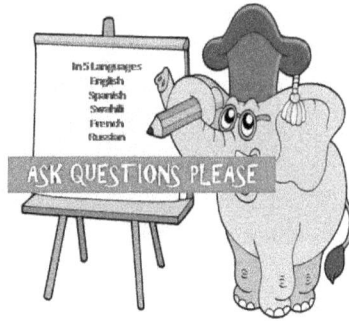

In 5 Languages
English
Spanish
Swahili
French
Russian

ASK QUESTIONS PLEASE

English-Español-Kiswahili-Français-Русскиий

ASK QUESTIONS

PLEASE

FRENCH

470

Lois McNeil était professeur de droit à l'École de droit Widespread où elle enseignait le droit de l'environnement.

Souvent après ses nombreuses conférences, Lois demandait à la classe, s'ils avaient des questions.

La plupart du temps, la classe de Lois serait harmonieusement répondre NON.

Cela dérangeait parfois Lois, comme elle se savait étudiante en droit une fois, qu'il y avait des centaines de fois où elle ne comprenait pas complètement ce qui lui était enseigné, c'était en posant des questions que Lois pouvait finalement comprendre la leçon.

Pas de questions, avant de continuer, Lois demandé à plusieurs reprises.

Il y eut un moment de silence qui indiqua que personne n'avait rien à dire.

Puis, tout à coup, le jeune homme assis à l'arrière de la classe, leva la main et dit:

J'ai une question.

Enfin, Lois répondit.

Je commençais à penser que j'étais dans une salle pleine de génies qui savaient tout.

Je suis heureux de savoir que je suis nécessaire, dit Lois.

Comment puis-je vous aider, monsieur Porter, demanda Lois.

M. Porter a commencé à poser sa question.

Après que M. Porter ait posé sa question, certains des autres étudiants ont parlé en même temps et ont dit:

J'allais poser la même question.

Lois répondit à la question de M. Porter. Lois demanda à nouveau à la classe.

Quelqu'un at-il des questions?

Cette fois, plusieurs étudiants lèvent la main pour poser une question à Lois.

Ainsi Lois conclut, elle a réitéré sa déclaration et dit à la classe Poser des questions S'il vous plaît, parce que, en posant des questions vous acquérir des connaissances et la compréhension.

Thank You

For Purchasing This Book
In Your Purchase, You Are Celebrating With Me
The Completion Of One Of God's Many Works
Through Me.

This Book Represents, The Completion Of Writing
700 Children's Books In 60 Days. 100 Of Which,
Are Written In 5 Different Languages

Contact Information

Website:
Booksspeakforyou.com
@Booksspeakforu (twitter)
1-800-757-0598
Email:
Booksspeakforyou@yahoo.com
School Visits:
cupcakeswithconversations.com
Author Contact: 267-318-8933

www.ingramcontent.com/pod-product-compliance
Lightning Source LLC
Chambersburg PA
CBHW071801020426

42331CB00008B/2357